I Have a Dream

Martin Luther King and the fight for Equal Rights

ANITA GANERI

W

FRANKLIN WATTS

LONDON • SYDNEY

First published in 2013 by Franklin Watts

Copyright © Franklin Watts 2013

Franklin Watts
338 Euston Road
London NW1 3BH

Franklin Watts Australia
Level 17/207 Kent Street
Sydney, NSW 2000

A CIP catalogue record for this book
is available from the British Library.

Dewey no: 973

ISBN: 978 1 4451 2358 5

Printed in China.

Franklin Watts is a division of Hachette Children's Books, an Hachette UK company.

www.hachette.co.uk

Series editor: Sarah Ridley
Editor in chief: John C. Miles
Designer: Jason Billin
Art director: Peter Scoulding
Picture research: Diana Morris

CONTENTS

Martin Luther King

Martin Luther King, civil rights leader.

On the evening of 4 April 1968, Martin Luther King Jr was shot dead as he stood on his motel balcony in Memphis, Tennessee. His murder sent shockwaves around the world and riots broke out in many US cities. Only 39 years old, he had already become the greatest leader of the civil rights movement in the USA, inspiring millions of people through his message of non-violent protest, and his outstanding speaking ability. A committed Christian, Martin Luther King had led campaigns and suffered prison sentences, all in the cause of the struggle for freedom and equality for all Americans.

In the 1950s and 60s, civil rights had become an issue of national concern in the USA. In the southern states, there were strict segregation laws in place, and black people were treated like second-class citizens. At home in Atlanta, Georgia, Martin experienced racial discrimination from an early age.
In 1955, when he was working as a pastor, he was asked to lead a boycott of the city buses in Montgomery, Alabama, after a black woman was arrested for refusing to give up her seat to a white passenger. This was the beginning of his serious involvement in the civil rights movement and of his historic struggle to bring about equality and justice for all Americans, black and white.

Martin Luther King, his wife, Coretta, and three of their four children.

"History has thrust upon me a responsibility from which I cannot turn away." Martin Luther King 1959

5

The childhood home of Martin Luther King.

Martin Luther King Jr was born on 15 January 1929, in Atlanta, Georgia, the second child of Alberta Williams King and Martin Luther King Sr. His father was the pastor of the nearby Ebenezer Baptist Church, and the Christian faith was a central part of family life. The Kings lived in a large, two-storey house but Martin's father had not always been so well off. His parents were very poor. Martin Sr was determined to better himself and had worked by day and attended school and college at night, in order to become a minister. He encouraged his own children to study hard at school and college.

At that time, strict segregation laws were in place in Atlanta. There were separate schools, theatres, restaurants and even drinking fountains for black and white people. Martin became aware of segregation from a young age, when two white friends were forbidden from playing with him because he was black.

Martin's father hated the system and refused to accept it. One day, he took his son to buy some shoes. When the white shop assistant asked them to sit at the back of the shop, in the area reserved for blacks, Martin's father refused and walked out. These, and other incidents, made a powerful impression on Martin.

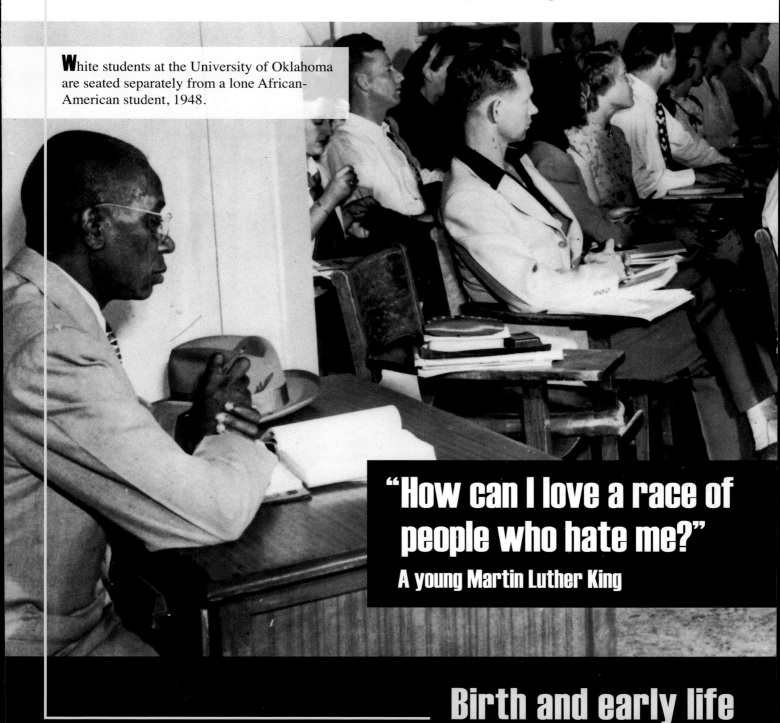

White students at the University of Oklahoma are seated separately from a lone African-American student, 1948.

"How can I love a race of people who hate me?"
A young Martin Luther King

Birth and early life

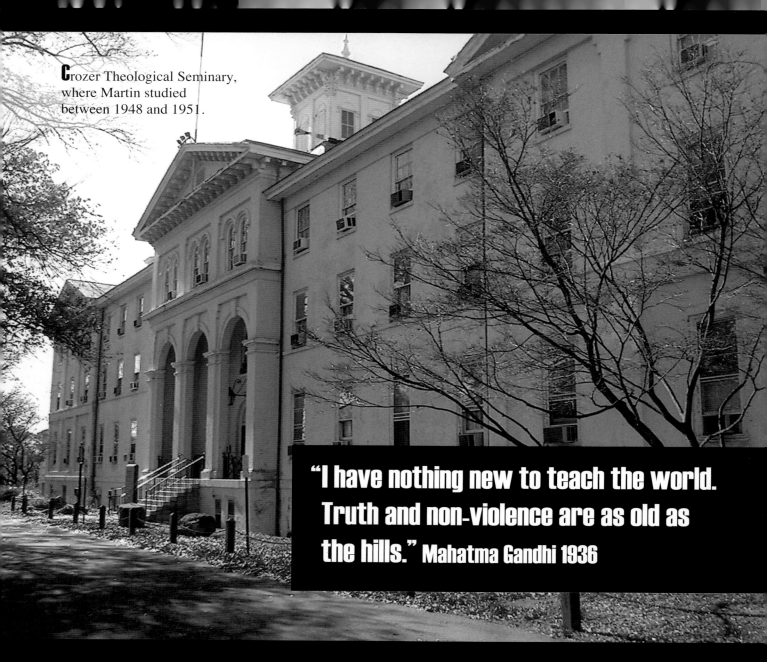

Crozer Theological Seminary, where Martin studied between 1948 and 1951.

"I have nothing new to teach the world. Truth and non-violence are as old as the hills." Mahatma Gandhi 1936

A brilliant student, Martin skipped several school years, and in 1944, aged just 15, entered Morehouse College to study for a degree in sociology. Martin soon realised that he wanted to become a minister of the church, like his father. Nervously, he delivered a trial sermon at his father's church. It was a huge success, and he was ordained in 1947. After graduation, Martin went to Crozer Theological Seminary in Pennsylvania. There, he began to think about the best way to end the evil of segregation. He found the answer in the works of American thinker, Henry David Thoreau, and Indian leader, Mahatma Gandhi. Both men taught that the most powerful weapon against injustice was non-violent civil disobedience.

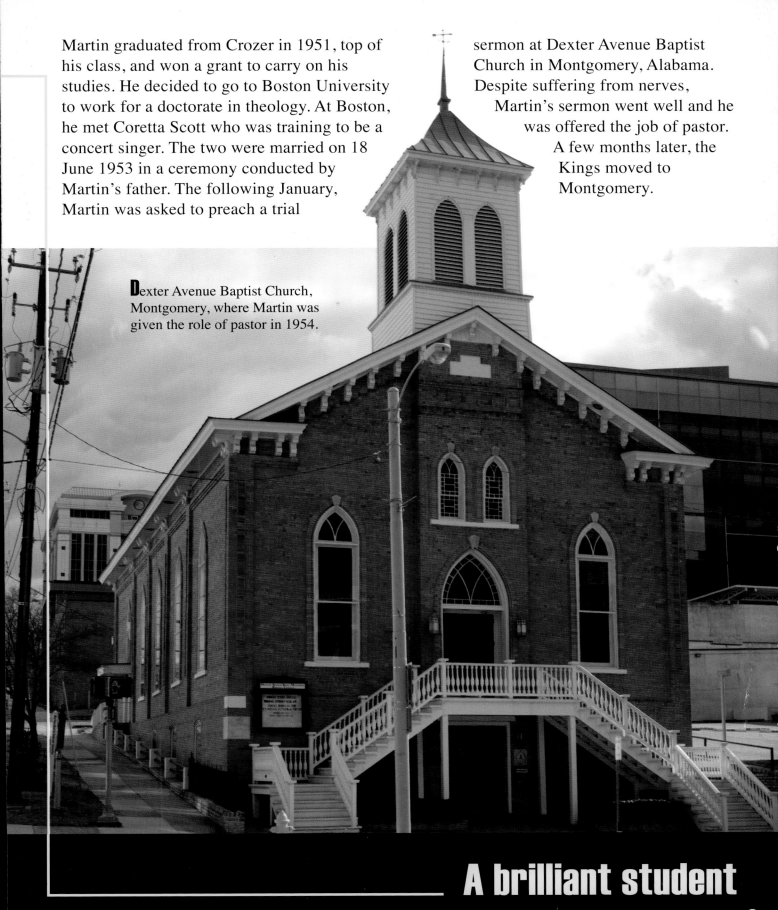

Martin graduated from Crozer in 1951, top of his class, and won a grant to carry on his studies. He decided to go to Boston University to work for a doctorate in theology. At Boston, he met Coretta Scott who was training to be a concert singer. The two were married on 18 June 1953 in a ceremony conducted by Martin's father. The following January, Martin was asked to preach a trial sermon at Dexter Avenue Baptist Church in Montgomery, Alabama. Despite suffering from nerves, Martin's sermon went well and he was offered the job of pastor. A few months later, the Kings moved to Montgomery.

Dexter Avenue Baptist Church, Montgomery, where Martin was given the role of pastor in 1954.

A brilliant student

1 December 1955

Rosa Parks, who refused to give up her seat for a white passenger.

Montgomery was a strictly segregated city and, to the Kings' dismay, many black people seemed afraid of challenging the system. Even on the city's buses, strict segregation occurred. There were no black bus drivers in the city, and many white drivers were hostile to their black passengers.

Furthermore, black people could only sit at the back of the bus and, if the whites-only section was full, they were forced to give up their seats. Then, on 1 December 1955, a black woman, called Rosa Parks, was arrested for refusing to give up her seat for a white passenger. The news spread like wildfire.

Black leaders called for a boycott of the city's buses. Martin became involved, offering his church as a meeting place. It was agreed that black people would boycott the buses for one day, on Monday 5 December. Volunteers started handing out leaflets – everything was set. But Martin was anxious. Would people have the courage to follow the boycott through? He need not have worried. There was a bus stop just outside the Kings' house and, on Monday morning, they watched as the first bus drove past. It was empty. The next bus was also empty, and the third had only two white passengers.

Black students cheer as an empty bus drives past. The bus company lost more and more money as the boycott took hold.

"We got to boycott the buses... Make it clear... we ain't taking this type of treatment any more."
E D Nixon, black civil rights leader 1955

Arrest of Rosa Parks

Reverand Ralph Abernathy talks to a reporter as he and Martin Luther King arrive for a meeting during the Montgomery bus boycott, 1956.

It was the same story all over the city – instead of using buses, black people walked, took cabs, and even rode on mules. That afternoon, Martin was elected president of the MIA (Montgomery Improvement Association), an organisation set up to head the bus boycott. The question was: what to do next? Should they extend the boycott or call it off? They decided to let the people decide. At a meeting, attended by over 4,000 people, Martin gave his most stirring speech so far. He called people to action but warned that this must be legal and non-violent. At the end, every single person stood up to vote in favour of the boycott continuing.

The MIA leaders set up a car pool to transport black people to and from work. More than 300 drivers offered their services but the city authorities soon began to get tough. They arrested drivers, including Martin, on the least pretence. The Kings also received threatening letters and phone calls, and in January 1956, their house was bombed. Luckily, no one was hurt. Despite this, the boycott continued, and finally, on 20 December 1956, the order came from the US Supreme Court to end bus segregation. The next morning, Martin and other leaders rode on the first integrated bus in Montgomery. The boycott had been a huge success.

"If we are wrong, God Almighty is wrong."
Martin Luther King 1955

Martin riding on the first integrated bus in Montgomery.

End of the bus boycott

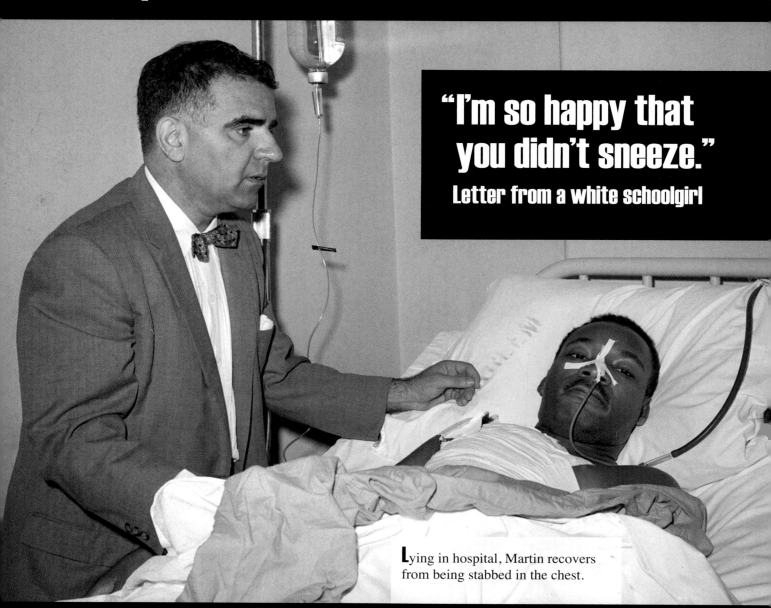

"I'm so happy that you didn't sneeze."
Letter from a white schoolgirl

Lying in hospital, Martin recovers from being stabbed in the chest.

After the bus boycott, Martin's fame spread far and wide. In 1957, he was elected president of the Southern Christian Leadership Conference (SCLC) which began a 'Crusade for Citizenship' to secure better voting rights for black people. Martin travelled up and down the country, giving speeches. He also found time to write a book about the bus boycott, called *Stride Toward Freedom*. On 20 September 1958, he was signing copies in a bookshop in New York when an insane woman stabbed him in the chest with a letter opener. An emergency operation saved his life but doctors said that, if he had sneezed, the letter opener would have killed him.

Towards the end of 1959, Martin made a life-changing decision. With great sadness, he told the members of his Montgomery church that he would soon be leaving. In order to reduce his huge workload, he was going to return to his hometown of Atlanta. There, he could devote more time to the SCLC and the struggle for civil rights. He told his congregation: "History has thrust upon me a responsibility from which I cannot turn away. I have no choice but to free you now." The Kings moved back to Atlanta in early 1960, and Martin became co-pastor, with his father, at Ebenezer Baptist Church.

Martin continued to deliver stirring sermons at Ebenezer Baptist Church, Atlanta.

Early 1960 Back to Atlanta

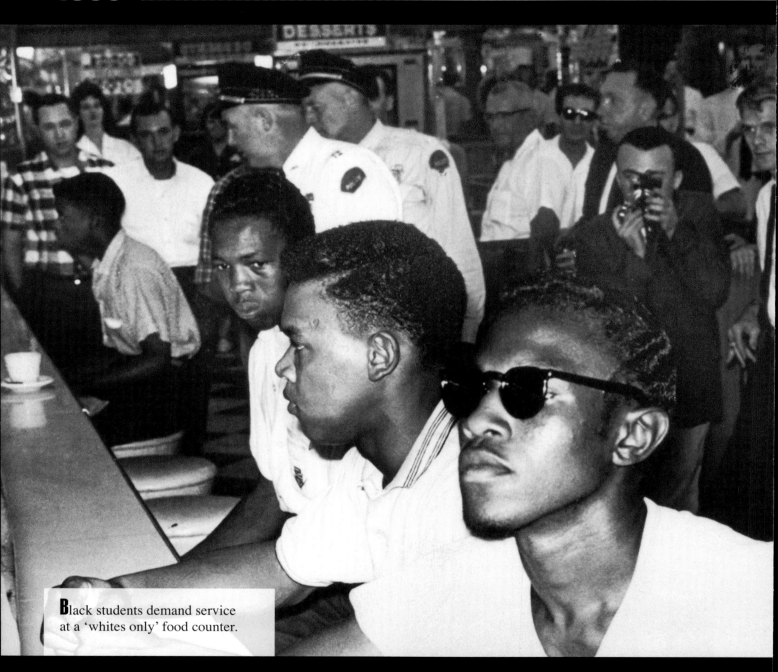

Black students demand service at a 'whites only' food counter.

At the time of the Kings' return to Atlanta, the civil rights movement was beginning to pick up speed in the south. On 2 February 1960, four black college students in Greensboro, North Carolina, marched into a Woolworth's store, sat down at the whites-only lunch counter and refused to leave until they were served. Over the next week, hundreds of other students, including some from white colleges, followed their example. Soon, the sit-ins spread to other parts of the south, and to theatres, libraries and supermarkets. Many of the students were arrested and put in jail.

As the sit-ins spread, Martin received many letters from students, asking for help and advice. Before long, he was taking an active part. On 19 October 1960, Martin and several students were arrested during a sit-in at a department store in Atlanta. A few days later, the students were released but Martin was promptly rearrested on a technicality, found guilty and sentenced to four months' hard labour. A few days later, he was suddenly released. He learnt that John F Kennedy and Kennedy's brother, Robert, had intervened on his behalf. That November, John F Kennedy won the US presidential election with three-quarters of the black vote.

Martin Luther King and other protestors are led from a department store by police detectives after a protest sit-in, 1960.

"For [Senator Kennedy] to be that courageous shows that he is really acting upon principle and not expediency."
Martin Luther King 1960

Student sit-ins

Martin and other protestors are arrested again in Albany, 1962.

In December 1961, Martin received an urgent phone call from a young black man, William G Anderson, leader of a protest group in Albany, Georgia. Hoping to rally the people, Anderson asked Martin to visit Albany to speak at a mass meeting. Martin agreed and spoke to an enthusiastic crowd at Shiloh Baptist Church. Next day, on 16 December, he led a march through the streets of Albany, demanding an end to segregation. The police were waiting. They arrested all the marchers, Martin included. The following July, Martin returned to Albany, only for the same thing to happen again. It soon became clear that the Albany protests had failed.

Martin now turned his attention to one of the most segregated cities in the USA – Birmingham, Alabama. There, black people faced violence and brutality on a daily basis, and even white people who opposed the system were too afraid to speak out. The city's police commissioner, Eugene 'Bull' Connor, was well known for his racist views, and prided himself on keeping black people 'in their place'. Martin and the other SCLC leaders drew up a careful plan. He called the campaign 'Project C', with the 'C' standing for 'Confrontation'. It began quietly enough, on 3 April, with a few sit-ins at the city's lunch counters.

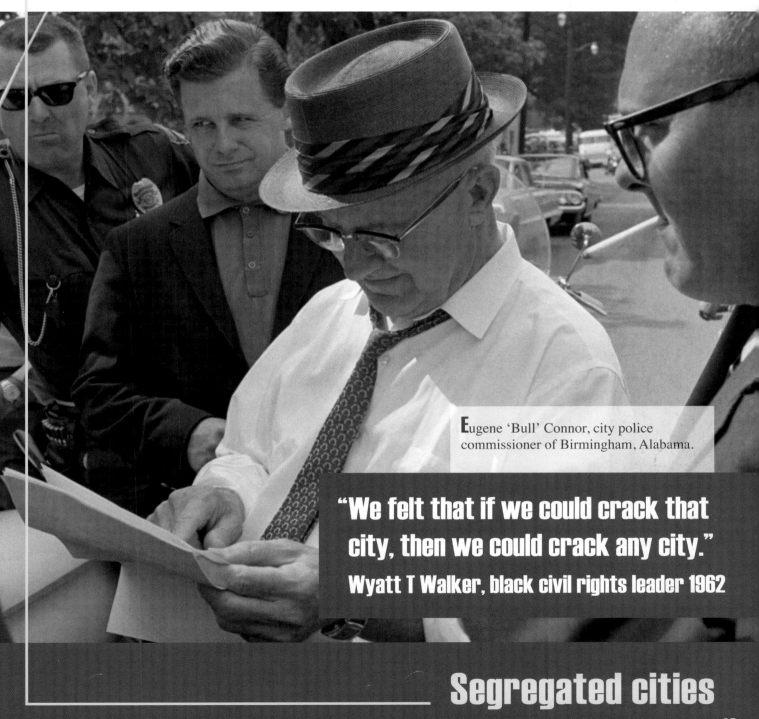

Eugene 'Bull' Connor, city police commissioner of Birmingham, Alabama.

"We felt that if we could crack that city, then we could crack any city."
Wyatt T Walker, black civil rights leader 1962

Segregated cities

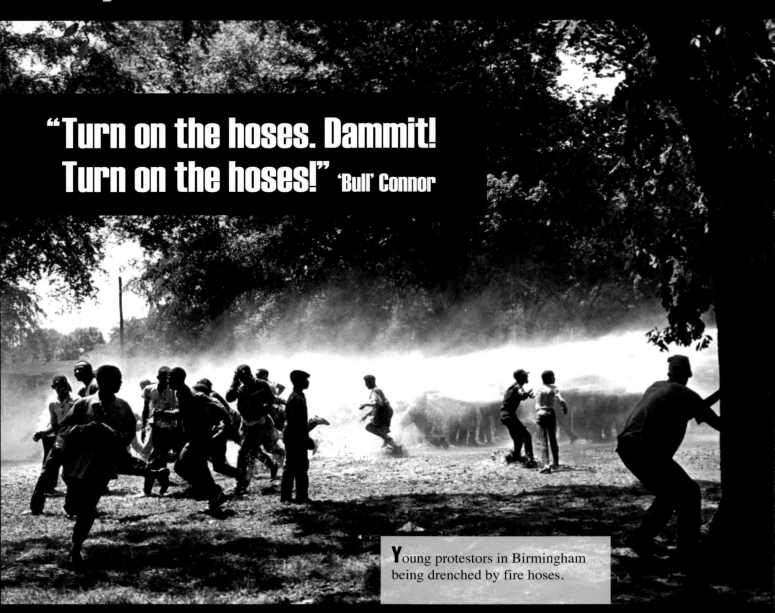

"Turn on the hoses. Dammit! Turn on the hoses!" 'Bull' Connor

Young protestors in Birmingham being drenched by fire hoses.

Over the next few weeks, the SCLC stepped up their campaign. The protests grew larger every day, and the city's jails filled up quickly, with Martin among those arrested. This time, he was placed in solitary confinement. Alone, in a dark cell, he began to despair. Meanwhile, back home in Atlanta, Coretta was worried. Unusually, she had not heard from Martin for two days. She decided that she had to do something and phoned President John F Kennedy asking for his help. Conditions improved immediately for Martin, and, after eight days, he was freed. Now he took the bold step of asking for volunteers from schools and colleges to come forward to join the campaign.

On 2 May 1963, a thousand young black people marched through Birmingham. The police arrested 900 of them. Another march followed the next day, with more than twice the number of protestors. This time, 'Bull' Connor had had enough and decided to get tough. He ordered his men to turn fire hoses on the marchers, and to let loose their police dogs.

Next morning, the papers were full of shocking pictures of young people being knocked down and brutally attacked. A few days later, Birmingham's business leaders met the SCLC for talks. They agreed to the demands for desegregation – the battle to desegregate Birmingham had been won.

Martin addresses the crowds during the Birmingham protests.

The battle for Birmingham

Martin Luther King and other civil rights activists were invited to meet with President John F Kennedy in 1963.

Throughout the summer of 1963, civil rights protests continued to grow. In the White House, President Kennedy asked Congress to pass a Civil Rights Bill to end segregation, and bring justice and equality. Not everyone shared his views. In June, the prominent African-American leader, Medgar Evers, was shot dead by a white man in front of his house. In the hope of putting pressure on Congress to pass the Civil Rights Bill, the SCLC and other groups planned a mass march on Washington DC on 28 August, at which Martin would speak. The march organisers estimated that about 100,000 people would attend the march, but they were stunned by the eventual size of the crowd.

On the morning of 28 August, at least 250,000 people arrived in Washington DC. They were black, white, old, young, teachers, ministers, farmers and even famous singers and film stars. At the Lincoln Memorial, they spilled onto the lawns and began to listen to the speakers. Martin was the last to speak. He had prepared his speech the night before and started off reading from it. But, seeing the huge crowd before him, he abandoned his script and began to speak from the heart. The speech he gave that day has become one of the most famous of all time. Broadcast on live television, it reached millions of viewers.

Martin Luther King (centre left) walks at the front of marchers as they enter Washington DC, August 1963.

March on Washington

"I have a dream that, one day, this nation will rise up and live out the true meaning of its creed: 'We hold these truths to be self-evident; that all men are created equal.'

I have a dream that, one day, on the red hills of Georgia, the sons of former slaves and the sons of former slave owners will be able to sit down together at the table of brotherhood.

I have a dream that, one day, even the state of Mississippi, a state sweltering with the heat of injustice, sweltering with the heat of oppression, will be transformed into an oasis of freedom and justice.

I have a dream that my four little children will, one day, live in a nation where they will not be judged by the color of their skin but by the content of their character.

"I have a dream today!

... I have a dream that, one day, every valley shall be exalted, every hill and mountain shall be made low, the rough places will be made plain and the crooked places will be made straight, and the glory of the Lord shall be revealed, and all flesh shall see it together. This is our hope. This is the faith that I will go back to the south with. With this faith, we will be able to hew out of the mountain of despair a stone of hope."

A huge crowd of more than 250,000 fills the lawns around the reflecting pool at the Lincoln Memorial, as Martin Luther King steps forward to speak.

"I have a *dream* today!"

"I have a dream"

Protestors cheer at the end of Martin's famous speech.

When Martin had finished speaking, he stepped down from the podium, to the deafening sound of roars and cheers from the crowd. Some people were crying. All those present, and the millions more watching on TV, knew that they had witnessed an historic moment. Afterwards, there was a reception in the White House. "I have a dream," President Kennedy told Martin, as he shook his hand. Martin was elated. Next day, newspapers at home and around the world carried reports of the march and quotes from Martin's speech. That summer, the civil rights cause moved forward faster than it had for many years.

On Sunday, 15 September, Martin was preaching at Ebenezer Baptist Church when devastating news came from Birmingham. A bomb had been thrown into the Sixteenth Street Baptist Church, killing four young girls and injuring many others. Filled with grief and despair, Martin rushed to the scene and was horrified by what he saw. A member of the local Klu Klux Klan was later arrested but released. (Years later, he was rearrested and convicted of murder.) At the funeral for three of the girls, Martin gave the eulogy. He told mourners that the girls had not died in vain – they would be remembered as heroines.

"My God, we're not even safe in church!"

Church-goer in Birmingham 1963

Crowds gather at the funeral of the girls killed in the bombing of the Birmingham church.

Washington and afterwards

Dr King watches as President Johnson signs the Civil Rights Bill.

"Let us close the springs of racial poison...
Let us make our nation whole."
President Lyndon B Johnson 1964

Two months later, another shocking act of violence rocked the country. On 22 November 1963, President John F Kennedy was shot dead by a sniper in Dallas. Martin was sickened and stunned. The country had not only lost a great leader but a strong supporter of civil rights. Martin blamed the President's death on a 'climate of hate'. To honour Kennedy's memory, President Lyndon B Johnson pressed Congress to pass the Civil Rights Bill as soon as possible. On 2 July 1964, Martin and other civil rights leaders were present in the White House as President Johnson signed the bill and turned it into law.

By now, Martin's fame had spread far and wide. He won many awards and prizes, both in the USA and abroad. Then, in October 1964, news came that he had won the Nobel Prize for Peace, the highest honour of all. In December, Martin flew to Oslo to receive his prize from the King of Norway. In his acceptance speech, he paid tribute to all of the millions of people who had fought for justice using non-violent means. "Yet when the years have rolled past…," he said, "men and women will know and children will be taught that we have a finer land… because these humble children of God were willing to suffer for righteousness' sake."

"It made me feel very humble indeed."

Martin Luther King

Acts and awards

Martin Luther King (right) faces Sheriff Jim Clark, Selma, 1965.

In early 1965, Martin took the fight for justice to the town of Selma, Alabama. The campaign was nicknamed 'Project Alabama'. Although every US citizen had the right to vote, many black people were denied that right due to impossible literacy tests they couldn't pass or taxes that they couldn't afford to pay. In Selma, more than half of the population was black, yet black people only accounted for one voter in every hundred. On 18 January, Martin arrived in Selma to lead a march to the courthouse. But he faced a powerful enemy in Jim Clark, the town's sheriff. Clark, a staunch racist, was determined to use brutal police tactics to 'preserve the white way of life'.

In February, a black marcher was shot by police during a peaceful protest in a nearby town. He died a few days later. Martin announced that he was stepping up the campaign with a mass protest march from Selma to Montgomery on Sunday 7 March. Despite the march being banned by the Alabama governor, more than 500 people set off. They did not get far. Just outside the town, they were met by a wall of state troopers, standing three deep across Highway 80. When the marchers refused to turn back, the police attacked with whips, clubs and tear gas. More than 140 people were injured in the vicious assault.

A marcher lies on the road, injured by the violent police treatment.

"Please, no! God, we're being killed."

Black marcher in Selma 1965

21 – 25 March 1965

A grim-faced Dr King leads marchers away from Selma.

News of the brutal attack shocked the American public as no other event in the civil rights struggle had before. Martin called on the country's religious leaders to join him and hundreds of others on another, so-called 'ministers' march'. That night, three white ministers who supported the campaign were assaulted by white racists. One of them,

Reverend James Reeb, later died. His murder caused outrage. President Johnson addressed the nation, calling for calm and vowing to push forward a new law, to remove all remaining barriers which prevented black voters from registering. He ordered the governor to allow the Selma to Montgomery march to take place under police protection.

On Sunday 21 March 1965, Martin led more than 3,000 marchers from Selma, along Highway 80. The march to Montgomery took five days. On 25 March, the marchers reached the Alabama State Capitol in Montgomery, where Martin petitioned the governor for black voting rights. The governor refused to see him but, in the White House, President Johnson could not ignore the issue any longer. He asked Congress to pass a new Voting Rights Bill. In August, the bill became the Voting Rights Act of 1965. The act made it illegal for black people in the southern states to be prevented from registering to vote. Martin flew to Washington for the official signing.

President Johnson presents Martin Luther King with the pen used to sign the Voting Rights Act.

> "It is wrong – dead wrong – to deny any of your fellow Americans the right to vote."
> President Johnson 1965

Selma to Montgomery

A poor black neighbourhood in Chicago in the 1960s.

After the success of Project Alabama, Martin turned his attention for the first time from the south to the cities of the north. In January 1966, he announced the start of the 'Chicago Campaign' to demand better living conditions for black people there. Many of them were desperately poor and had badly paid jobs, or no jobs at all. Martin moved his family into a cramped, cold apartment in a poor black neighbourhood, known as 'Slumdale'. He spent the next few months touring the black neighbourhoods, even visiting Chicago's notorious youth gangs. He was appalled by the terrible conditions that he found.

On 10 July, 'Freedom Sunday', more than 30,000 people gathered at Soldier Field to hear Martin give a rousing speech. Afterwards, he stuck a list of demands on the door of City Hall. Next day, he presented the demands to Mayor Daley in person. If Daley did not act, Martin promised to launch a whole series of protests. Then, disaster struck. Rioting broke out in Chicago's West Side, triggered by the sweltering summer heat. In August, Martin led another march. White onlookers pelted the marchers with missiles – a brick hit Martin on the head – but, finally, on 26 August, Daley agreed to meet Martin for talks. This resulted in an agreement that fairer housing and equal rights would be the city's top priorities.

Martin leads a march to campaign for social change in Chicago.

"Oh, I've been hit so many times I'm immune to it."
Martin Luther King 1966

The Chicago Campaign

Martin Luther King, about to board the flight to Memphis in April 1968.

At the beginning of 1968, Martin was busy planning another march on Washington DC for April, as part of a 'Poor People's Campaign'. But first, he headed to Memphis, Tennessee, where the city's refuse workers, most of them black, had gone out on strike. Martin wanted to help them win better pay and working conditions and agreed to lead a mass protest march on 5 April. He arrived in Memphis on 3 April, after his flight had been delayed by a bomb threat, causing the plane to be closely guarded overnight. Martin, who had faced many threats to his life over the years, shrugged this one off.

In Memphis, Martin and Ralph Abernathy checked into Room 306 of the Lorraine Motel. That evening, Martin addressed a crowd of about 2,000 people at the Bishop Mason Temple. In a stirring speech, he spoke about the struggle ahead. Towards the end, he talked about being stabbed in New York and the threats to his life. "But it really doesn't matter to me now," he said, "because I have been to the mountaintop... And I've looked over. And I've seen the Promised Land." Many people who heard the speech were convinced that Martin knew that he would be killed. It was the last speech he ever made.

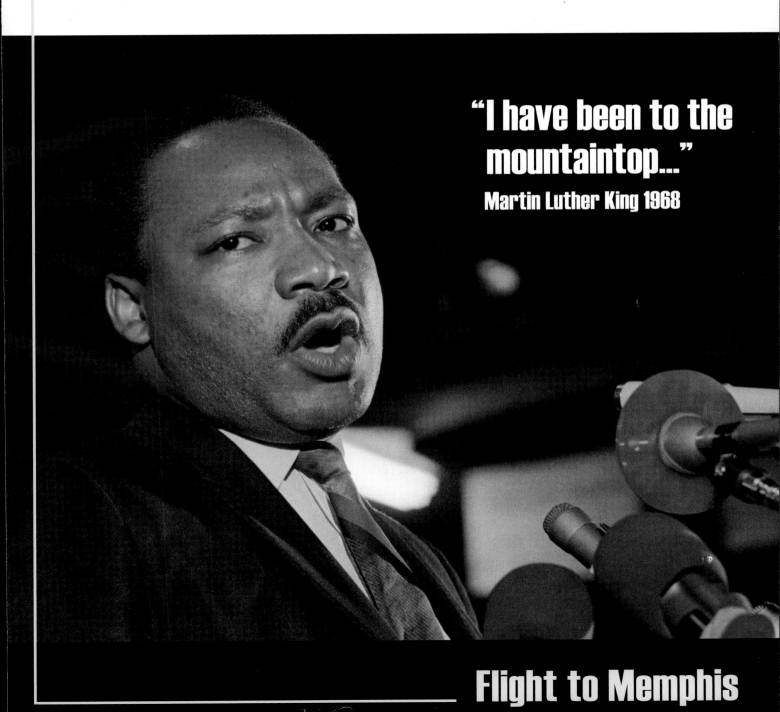

"I have been to the mountaintop..."

Martin Luther King 1968

Flight to Memphis

Martin and Abernathy on the balcony of the Lorraine Motel, Memphis, the day before the fatal shooting.

Next morning, Martin met with his colleagues at the motel to discuss the forthcoming march. After lunch, he spent time with his brother who was also staying there. Their conversation turned to their evening plans. Martin and his staff had all been invited out for dinner at a local

Later, Martin changed his clothes, then went to stand outside on the balcony while he waited for the others. The evening was chilly so Solomon Jones, Martin's driver, went inside to fetch Martin's coat. Suddenly, there was a rifle shot. A bullet tore into Martin's face with such force that it knocked

Ralph Abernathy, who had heard the shot, rushed out of the hotel room to find Martin crumpled on the ground. An ambulance was called, but, despite the doctors' best efforts, Martin died an hour later in St Joseph's Hospital. "I'm sorry," the head surgeon told Abernathy, "but we've lost him. It's over."

Martin was 39 years old. His murder left his family and friends shattered, and caused shock, grief and anger across the country and abroad. President Johnson declared 7 April a national day of mourning. A white convict, James Earl Ray, was later arrested for the shooting, and sentenced to life in prison.

"Oh my God! Martin's been shot."
Ralph Abernathy

Next day, the national and international papers were full of reports about Martin's death.

A fatal bullet

Martin Luther King's coffin is loaded aboard an aeroplane for the flight to Atlanta.

Martin's body was flown home to Atlanta to lie in state. Thousands of mourners filed past his coffin to pay their last respects. On 9 April, his funeral was held in Ebenezer Baptist Church. The church was packed, with tens of thousands more people standing outside, listening to the service over loudspeakers. They heard a tape recording of Martin's own words: "If any of you are around when I have to meet my day, I don't want a long funeral. And if you get somebody to deliver the eulogy, tell him not to talk too long… I'd like someone to mention that day that Martin Luther King Jnr tried to give his life serving others. I'd like for somebody to say that Martin Luther King Jnr tried to love somebody."

Afterwards, his coffin was placed on a farm cart, pulled by two mules, a symbol of his Poor People's Campaign. Then, with some 50,000 people following behind, and millions more watching on TV, his body was taken to South View Cemetery, where he was buried near his grandparents. "The grave is too narrow for his soul," Ralph Abernathy said, "but we commit his body to the ground." His gravestone had his name and the dates of his birth and death. Underneath were the words of an old African-American hymn which he had quoted many times: "Free at last, free at last. Thank God Almighty, I'm free at last."

"Thank God Almighty, I'm free at last."
African-American hymn

REV. MARTIN LUTHER KING, JR.
1929 — 1968
*"Free at last, Free at last,
Thank God Almighty
I'm Free at last."*

CORETTA SCOTT KING
1927 — 2006
*"And now abide Faith, Hope,
Love, These Three; but the
greatest of these is Love."*
1 Cor. 13:13

Despite the work of Martin and others in the civil rights movement, it continues to be more difficult for a black American to succeed in life than for a white American of equal education.

By the time of his death, Martin had already helped to change the situation for black people in American society. Many cities had been forced to abandon their rules on segregation, and black people were now able to exercise their right to vote. He had also tried to show people that the best way to bring about change was through non-violent means. This was a much more powerful weapon than violence could ever be. After Martin's death, the civil rights movement continued, working to bring about justice and equality for everyone, regardless of their colour, religion or race.

In the USA today, black and white people are equal under the law, though problems still remain. Often, white people have better-paid jobs, more opportunities, and live in better homes and neighbourhoods than black people, and there are still many cases of racial prejudice. Many black people have achieved high office, however. In 2008, Barack Obama became the first African-American to be elected as President of the USA. On the eve of his inauguration in Washington DC, he remembered Martin Luther King, saying: "Tomorrow, we will come together as one people on the same mall where Dr King's dream echoes still." Obama was re-elected for a second term in 2012.

Fruits of the non-violent struggle

Nelson Mandela was released from prison in 1990 after 27 years of captivity.

Other world leaders have also been inspired by Martin's example. From 1948 to 1994, a system of racial segregation, called apartheid, was in place in South Africa. Black civil-rights leaders, such as Nelson Mandela, spent many years in jail. In 1994, South Africa held its first multi-racial elections, with black people allowed to vote for the first time. Mandela won a landslide victory and became the country's first black president. In his victory speech, he included Martin's words: "You have shown such a calm, patient determination to reclaim this country as your own, and now we can loudly proclaim from the rooftops – Free at last! Free at last!"

Martin's wife, Coretta Scott King, remained active in the civil rights movement until her death in 2006. After his death, she established the King Center for Non-violent Social Change in Atlanta, as a lasting memorial to her husband. In 1980, Martin's birthplace, church and burial site in Atlanta were designated as the Martin Luther King Jnr National Historic Site. In 1983, the US Congress passed a bill to create a national holiday – Martin Luther King Day. It is celebrated on the third Monday in January, close to Martin's birthday. In some places, it is marked with speeches and peaceful marches, remembering Martin's guiding dream of a 'colour-blind' society.

A march on Martin Luther King Day.

Glossary

activist Someone actively involved in a cause.

apartheid A system of government in South Africa in which black and white people were kept apart. Black people were treated as inferior to white people.

boycott Refusing to buy or use something as a means of protesting against an unfair situation.

civil disobedience Refusing to obey the law, pay taxes and so on as a means of political protest.

civil rights The rights of each person in a society to equality, regardless of race or gender, and to the right to vote.

Congress The law-making branch of the US government, consisting of the Senate and the House of Representatives.

creed A set of beliefs.

doctorate The highest type of degree awarded by a university or college.

eulogy A speech given in praise of a person, often at a funeral.

hard labour A prison sentence involving hard physical work.

integrated Mixing different groups of people together in society.

Ku Klux Klan An extreme, racist organisation from the USA. Members wore white costumes with white, pointed hats.

Lincoln Memorial A monument in Washington D.C. that houses a statue of Abraham Lincoln, the 16th president of the USA.

literacy Reading and writing.

lunch counter In the USA, the name for a small restaurant or food bar, serving light meals across a long counter.

motel A roadside hotel.

mules Animals that are crossbreeds between donkeys and horses.

ordained Appointed as a minister or priest in the Christian Church.

pastor A minister in a Christian Church.

petition Demand some form of action from a government body or other authority.

racial discrimination Treating people differently on the basis of their colour or race.

racist A person who treats other people differently and is prejudiced against them on the grounds of their colour or race.

registering Putting your name on a list to allow you to do something, such as vote.

segregation Keeping different groups of people apart, because of their race, religion or other differences.

seminary A college for the training of ministers and priests.

sermon A speech given as part of a religious service.

sniper A gunman who hides and fires from his or her hiding place.

sociology The study of human society and how it works.

solitary confinement When a prisoner is kept on his or her own for long periods of time, without contact with other people.

theology The study of religion.

White House The official residence and main office of the President of the USA.

http://www.thekingcenter.org/

The website of the Martin Luther King Jr. Center for Nonviolent Social Change ('The King Center') which was established by Coretta King in 1968.

http://www.nps.gov/malu/index.htm

Learn about Martin Luther King's childhood home, the Ebenezer Baptist Church where he worshipped and preached, and the crypt where he is buried with Coretta in Atlanta.

https://www.morehouse.edu/kingcollection/index.php

The King Collection at Morehouse College includes many of Martin Luther King's own books, handwritten notes, speeches, sermons and memorabilia, such as travel tickets.

http://mlk-kpp01.stanford.edu/

Another collection of Martin Luther King's speeches and letters, as well as information about his life and work. The collection is managed by Stanford University.

http://www.nobelprize.org/nobel_prizes/peace/laureates/1964/king-bio.html#

The official website of the Nobel Prize, including information about Martin's award in 1964, including a video of him accepting the Nobel Prize for Peace from King Olaf of Norway.

Note to parents and teachers

Every effort has been made by the Publishers to ensure that the web sites in this book are suitable for children, that they are of the highest educational value, and that they contain no inappropriate or offensive material. However, because of the nature of the Internet, it is impossible to guarantee that the contents of these sites will not be altered. We strongly advise that Internet access is supervised by a responsible adult.

Index